# MODERN DAY
## *Courage*

JALENE E. MURPHY

◆ FriesenPress

One Printers Way
Altona, MB R0G 0B0
Canada

www.friesenpress.com

**Copyright © 2023 by Jalene E. Murphy**
First Edition — 2023

All rights reserved.

No part of this publication may be reproduced in any form, or by any means, electronic or mechanical, including photocopying, recording, or any information browsing, storage, or retrieval system, without permission in writing from FriesenPress.

Author photo by Jon Popowich

ISBN
978-1-03-916134-4 (Hardcover)
978-1-03-916133-7 (Paperback)
978-1-03-916135-1 (eBook)

*1. Biography & Autobiography, Personal Memoirs*

Distributed to the trade by The Ingram Book Company

*For the man who walked by my side for eighteen years—
Thank you for your endless love and gentle encouragement to
look within.*

Treaty No. 6 Territory [on the Prairies of Canada]. Thank
you for allowing me to work, live, think and write as a free
and independent woman. I am thankful for the peace and
freedom it has afforded me.

# TABLE OF CONTENTS

| | |
|---|---|
| Introduction | vii |
| Chapter 1  My Ruby Tuesday Dream | 1 |
| Chapter 2  Childfree and Awesome | 7 |
| Chapter 3  Jalene E. Murphy vs. Perfectionism | 13 |
| Chapter 4  Coming Home | 23 |
|     Part One  Connections | 23 |
|     Part Two  Mental Health and Healing | 33 |
|     Part Three  Always and Forever | 41 |
| A Heartfelt Thank You | 49 |

# INTRODUCTION

Taking the necessary steps to find your true self and live authentically can be scary. No, let me rephrase; it can be utterly terrifying. It was for me.

For years, I was in some ways living a life true to me. In other ways I wasn't. I really wasn't looking to find a better version of myself — in fact, I was staunchly assertive that I didn't need to change.

But then life took me down a path that showed me otherwise.

*Modern Day Courage* is a collection of stories about my journey of discovery. I have come to understand that sharing is essential to the human spirit. Stories connect us to each other and strengthen our collective hope in humanity. They make us feel we are not alone.

If you're reading this, you are likely already seeking something more from your life.

Finding your true self won't be easy. A million reasons exist for not taking the first step and a million more for turning back once you begin. No clear road map exists, and at times there will be perfect confusion. It will require hope and effort — an incredible amount of both.

The risk is huge, but the reward is incalculable.
Be gentle with yourself. It will take time.
Don't give up.

And above all, on those days when you do feel like surrendering, remember that you have a powerful ally to help you take the next step, . . . *Modern Day Courage.*

*Chapter 1*

# MY RUBY TUESDAY DREAM

Osâwahkesîs (o-s-uh-kay-sis) -Red Fox.

Red Fox symbolizes the strategy to achieve that dream. Red represents passion, strength, power, courage and is an exciting energy.

> *"A winner is a dreamer who never gives up".*
> South Africa Anti-apartheid revolutionary
> Nelson Mandela.

People around the planet have different dreams of how they want their world to look. Some dream of a better life for their children while others have dream jobs, dream homes, and dream vacations. Me? My dream was about five feet tall and six feet wide, and it came with a motor.

Growing up in the bite-size prairie town of Wetaskiwin, Alberta, with a population shy of 10,000 wasn't all that exciting for me. The city's chief claim to fame is Canada's oldest water tower. There was your normal small-town stuff — a library, schools, several churches, a movie theatre, a community pool, and hockey and curling rinks. The main street is aptly named "Historic Downtown". Railway tracks run smack through town, and long freight trains regularly blocked all four railway crossings going from the east side to the west side of town. Drive five minutes in any direction and you were probably on a dirt road in the midst of farmers' fields.

In 1997, I was in Grade 11 and planning my first international trip to England with the Wetaskiwin Composite High School extracurricular concert band. I was part of the crew in third chair position playing squeaky clarinet, and I was excited about my first opportunity to travel — I had never been on a plane before! The trip cost $1,200, which was a lot of money and an enormous obstacle. I didn't have a job, and my savings account at the credit union only held a few dollars. Asking my parents for help was pointless as I had five siblings, and Dad was the sole income earner. At the best of times, money was tight. I knew that the only way I was going on this trip was if I somehow paid my way.

Lucky for me I had a friend who worked part time at the Canadian Tire in the Wetaskiwin Mall, so in went my application and soon I landed my first job as a cashier, earning minimum wage of $4.25 an hour. I put in a lot of hours on the weekends, wearing that tacky red Canadian Tire polo shirt, and I eventually saved enough to pay for the trip. England, here I come!

It . . . . was . . . . love . . . . at . . . . first . . . . sight!

I stopped dead in my tracks when I spied an adorable, speedy, and pint-size car driving down a London lane. I came to know and learn about the Mini Cooper that day. It matched exactly how I felt, and it instantaneously became my dream car! The dream of one day owning an iconic, British-made Mini Cooper was conceived there and then.

Why did this mouse-sized car leave such an elephant-sized imprint on me? I felt I could relate to the Mini in so many ways.

Like the Mini, I am small in stature.

Like the Mini, I am driven.

Like the Mini, I am cute and peppy.

Owning a Mini meant having independence — I craved freedom and wanted to drive out of my small-town life.

Cars have always been a part of my life. Everyone I knew in Wetaskiwin owned a vehicle or two, and the city was famous for its "Auto-mile" of countless auto dealers. Everyone in the province was familiar with the advertising jingle, "Cars cost less in Wetaskiwin", but all that was available were the bland, plain-Jane models put out by Ford, GMC, Dodge, and Toyota. Occasionally we spied a BMW, Mercedes, or sporty Subaru — probably driven by a dentist or a lawyer — but that was it.

So, when I first saw the Mini Cooper, I wasn't prepared, and I had no defence against the emotions of "I desire, I want, I need, I gotta-have-this-one-day" that flooded my being. I might have been from a small prairie town, but it didn't stop me from dreaming big. As Kenyan-Mexican actress Lupita Nyong'o once said, "No matter where you're from, your dreams are valid".

How did my dream car come to be? A Mini-history lesson (pun intended).

In early 1957, the Suez Canal had been closed to shipping for five months, following Egypt's nationalisation of the Canal and the ensuing invasion by Israel, France, and England — also known as the Suez Crisis. By this time, two-thirds of Europe's oil passed through the Canal, so the closure caused huge fuel shortages, and car manufacturers tried to get more sensible about fuel consumption. Top engineer Alec Issigonis of the British Motor Corporation designed the small, economical, and fuel-efficient Morris Mini Minor that carried four adults. It went on sale in 1959 and was a big hit.

Issigonis's most important innovations were more passenger space and better handling. He pushed the wheels all the way out to the corners and turned the engine sideways, which made the interior roomier and provided increased stability. During the 1960s, the Mini Cooper, as it became known, was one of the most successfulb vehicles in motorsports, winning rallies, touring cups, and endurance races.

Since then, the Classic Mini Cooper has evolved and changed, and several new models have been added to the family. This has in no way diluted its spirit, and the constant innovation that characterizes the Mini will make it popular for years to come.

I returned to the Prairies, and for the next twenty-two years I nurtured the dream of owning a Mini. When the opportunity finally came to buy a car all on my own, there was no wavering as to what it would be. Yes, I could have bought the more sensibly priced Alero that my sister's neighbour was selling or my brother's second-hand Honda Civic. But I had eyes only for a Mini. My dad kept reminding me that a Mini was an import and would cost more for maintenance and repairs, but none of that mattered. When I thought of a Mini, I experienced the same joy in my heart as that day in London. That joy was my compass, and I knew I was headed in the right direction.

When I finally got behind the wheel of my red Mini-Cooper with black racing stripes — which I affectionately named Ruby — I was grinning ear to ear. I actually pinched myself a couple of times, as I realized my dream had become a beautiful, joyful reality.

Former First Lady of the United States and activist Eleanor Roosevelt once said, "The future belongs to those who believe in the beauty of their dreams".

At times dreams do not seem sensible, practical, or even tangible. But for twenty-two years I never stopped dreaming of owning a Mini Cooper. I knew one day I would be a winner, knowing that it didn't matter where I came from as I never lost sight of the beauty of my dream. Finally, it all came together, and I drove off in Ruby on a Tuesday!

## Chapter 2
## CHILDFREE AND AWESOME

Sawêyimêw (sah-way-I-may-ow) - Taking care/looking after someone.

Eagles represent love and belonging as well as an authoritative figure that looks after those they love or want to protect.

Brown represents dependability, security and safety.

Just because I have a uterus doesn't mean I have to use it for childbearing! But apparently, much of the world thinks otherwise.

"You are not complete unless you have children".
"Your husband doesn't want children?"
"The only fulfillment as a woman is to be a mother".
"You'll change your mind".

"It's selfish not to have kids".

And then the one I have heard the most — "Don't worry, there's still time".

Throughout the last twenty years, I've heard these comments with maybe the odd variation. The message is resoundingly clear. Women, especially after marriage, are expected to have children. As soon as I was married, people casually asked, "When are you buying your first home?" followed by, "When are you starting a family? How many children do you want?"

When I have told people I don't want children of my own, the reactions have varied. Some have felt insulted, and others dropped their jaws and were speechless. Often the body language tells me they feel sorry for me. When someone tells me that I'll change my mind, I'm both insulted and amused. How do they know what I want more than I do? My grandma questioned why I married if I wasn't going to have children. In her strict Catholic way of thinking, this was what was supposed to happen. It was the logical next step for her, but illogical to me. Sometimes I'm told that I am selfish. That baffles me. I think it's selfish when people have kids and then don't give them the love, time, and attention they need as they are too busy with their lives. Only once did a brave and honest soul mutter just loud enough for me to hear, "You're lucky".

For the fourteen years that I was married, I felt that my husband and I *were* a family. We didn't need children to fulfill the expectation of the traditional and nuclear family mindset. I truly loved our life and how it was set up. And so I feel that as much as motherhood is celebrated, so too should the choice not to have children. For me, it was a choice, a deliberate choice of how I wanted to live my life. I just couldn't see myself embracing motherhood wholeheartedly. And I see no shame in this.

Before I go any further, I have to say that I applaud those who lovingly choose the often difficult, unpaid career of being a full-time, hands-on parent. As a child, I saw firsthand how much time and money, endless effort, and love it takes to care properly for children. My mom and dad raised us six kids on a single teacher's income. Mom was a stay-at-home professional-league parent who worked tirelessly without a salary, overtime, sick days, and paid vacation, accumulating only a meager pension. It was relentless. While my parents loved us and would have agreed that having children was one of the most life-changing experiences a person could have, I came away from my childhood feeling that parenthood is not a decision that should be taken lightly.

My choice to remain child-free isn't without its benefits, as I enjoy freedoms that a parent can only dream of. In my case, it is the freedom to travel, which offers opportunities to learn and grow. I work in the travel industry, and so I take advantage of every opportunity to get on a plane. My husband and I visited Thailand for a month for our one-year wedding anniversary. Another month was spent living as beach bums on Big Corn Island in Nicaragua reading the classics that I have always wanted to read but never found time for. One April we lived in Paris, soaking up the French lifestyle and exploring cafés and galleries. Shorter, spur-of-the-moment trips have been possible as well, such as when I zipped off to Rome for a week after winning a pair of business-class tickets at work. And then there was my long-term travel goal that required four years of saving — visiting each continent before I turned forty years old. I even coined a new word to describe myself. I was a "Septacontinentalist!" All of this was possible only because I didn't have to juggle day care or schooling, be tied to a school calendar, and save for children's expenses.

While I am fortunate to have seen so much of our diverse and awe-inspiring world, I value even more the opportunity to foster deep, enduring relationships with my nieces and nephews. Aunthood rocks! Being child-free, I have time to support my nieces and nephews in many ways. I take this role to heart and attend track and field events, Christmas concerts, band recitals, basketball games, and Lunar New Year dance celebrations. I also share my passions with them, some of which — art, travel, fashion, and music — don't interest my siblings.

Some recent research supports the notion that aunts and uncles play an important role in the families of their siblings. In *The Forgotten Kin*, the first comprehensive study of aunts and uncles, Professor Robert M. Milardo explains that parents' siblings have the opportunity to wield a specific influence on children. "Their knowledge is unique, and to a certain extent, unburdened by the conventional expectation held of parents", he writes. "This may be especially true of childless aunts who are free to deviate from traditional views of mothering, domesticity, and femininity". He goes on to report:

> For childless siblings, the arrival of a niece or nephew can represent a welcome opportunity to engage with young children that might not otherwise be available and

occasion a closer bond between siblings. In a popular treatment of aunts, a childless aunt reckoned that with her niece, she was able to "receive and express the kind of unquestioning affection parents get to enjoy every day," and later added that "aunts can go home when the child gets testy". . . It is perhaps no accident that the most active aunts and uncles are often those who are relatively established, single, and childless.

When I think of the many experiences I have shared with my nieces and nephews, I am overwhelmed with emotions of joy and gratefulness. One of the most memorable was taking my four young nieces to the Winspear Center for the Edmonton Symphony Orchestra as they presented Disney in concert. The girls dressed up for the event and were giddy with excitement as we headed downtown for the musical extravaganza. There they learned about the two-minute bell to curtain call, how to match their tickets to their seat numbers, and how to welcome a conductor to the stage. That evening they were exposed to live music in a world-class venue. Who knows, they may develop a love for the symphony or simply the joy of live music.

I have also looked for opportunities to introduce them, especially Vanessa, to art events. Vanessa is especially creative and artsy, and together we have visited the Art Gallery of Alberta. I send her daily messages of art postings through Instagram and also took her to visit the gallery of world-renowned Indigenous artist Mr. Alex Janvier in Cold Lake, Alberta. It was a full-day trip from Edmonton north-east to Cold Lake, but I was excited to expose her to such a phenomenal contemporary painter and for the road trip-time together talking about art, eating our favourite road trip snacks all the while taking in the views of the Prairies. The trip was soul rewarding, and my heart was bursting at the seams as we stood side-by-side admiring the art on the gallery wall.

With Bonna, I incorporated my love of travel with her interest in baking by making Parisian croissants from scratch. Gathering the ingredients, the recipes to reference, and the accurate utensils — it was fun just getting to the starting line! It proved to be a tasty journey and a means of connecting and supporting each other as we learned something new together. Wishing one day to take her to Paris for a week of hands-on pastry training. I encourage all my nieces and nephews to dream big!

There are numerous ways to live a fruitful and loving life, and one of these is to be child-free and an active aunt. It makes for a life that I'm ecstatic to be living. Not everyone agrees with me or understands my decision, but I have battled with society's norms and my inner critic, and in the end I have chosen to honour what is right in my heart and then my head — I occupy both!

# Chapter 3
# JALENE E. MURPHY VS. PERFECTIONISM

Pakoseyimowin (pah-ko-say-m-ow-in)- Hope.

Dragonflies represent hope. They also represent change, a rebirth and a sense of insight.

Teal represents clarity, a feeling of balance, calm and tranquility.

"Ladies and Gentlemen, . . . Let's get ready to rumble!

"Welcome to the main event; the moment we have all been waiting for! To those here tonight and viewers tuning in around the world — thank you for joining us. What we are about to witness is a true battle of human behaviour.

"This real-life fight is steeped in anticipation and dripping with excitement.

"The two contenders: Jalene E. Murphy and Perfectionism.

"Can Perfectionism be fought and defeated in the clothes shopping arena? We will soon find out!

"One thing is for certain. In this twelve-month epic battle, we're going to see a lot of action, technique, and strategy. These two fighters have a deep-rooted and soul-numbing history. The truth is, they don't like each other, but they do respect each other.

"Perfectionism for sure has its allure and seductiveness. It's also elusive and sleek and wears many disguises as it camouflages easily into day-to-day life. Jalene has come up short against Perfectionism in previous bouts, but she has an unrelenting drive and won't be backing down easily. This will be a fight for the ages!

"The action is about to begin. ABC's Wide World of Sports introduction says it best — one contestant will have 'the thrill of victory' and the other 'the agony of defeat. This is the human drama of athletic competition!' And now we go ringside.

"Fighting out of the blue corner is the true underdog. SHE . . . IS . . . BACK! Hungry, scrappy, and ready to prove she has what it takes. She has been caught cold in the past, but tonight she is dead set on writing a different ending. Carrying the heart of a champion and spirit of a winner, she is primed to seize her first title. This is personal for her — a mental game fueled by sheer grit and backed with never-faltering and staggering determination. Standing at 5-foot-2 and weighing in at 110 lbs., make some noise for Jalene 'Rainbow Puncher' Murphy!

## MODERN DAY COURAGE

"The fighter in the red corner almost doesn't need an introduction as the undisputed, reigning, and undefeated champion of the world. Universally recognized with a perfect professional record in all seventeen weight classes and the best pound-for-pound fighter to date, this contestant is agile and one of the biggest stylists the ring has ever seen. We're confident we'll see the signature move of the quick jab causing a feeling of deflation and the showstopping notion of 'not-good-enough'.

A name that needs no introduction, put your hands together for the one, the only "Flawless Wonder" Perfectionism!

"What promises to be a spectacular fight will soon be underway. But first, let's hear from the contenders."

Flawless Wonder: "Yes! I have walked over Jalene for years. It's easy, as she is a sucker! She easily gets drawn into a match where she believes she is the exception and can win. She is super competitive, so it's comical watching her try! Jalene's big weakness is that she constantly needs outside validation. She takes a lot of pride in her appearance, but she is totally insecure and wants attention. She needs compliments and practically begs for flirty remarks to fuel her esteem. So that's how I get to her every time. I am insidious and unrelenting. I haunt her, I hound her, and I tear her down with perfectly placed thoughts of NOT GOOD ENOUGH! She is so feeble minded that she can't resist. Nothing brings me more pleasure when she is all worked up and goes out shopping thinking she is going to beat me by finding that perfect outfit. I roll on the floor laughing at how pitiful she is!"

Rainbow Puncher: "Oh, yeah, Perfectionism and I go way back! The Flawless Wonder has been whooping me in many areas of my life — shaking my self confidence, unsettling my peace of mind, and making me spend my hard-earned money! Trying to be perfect meant spending money to look my best in new clothes. Sometimes I spent a whole day going from store to store looking for the perfect outfit to match the shoes to match the jewellery and clutch for the big event. I felt judged for the clothes I wore. Perfectionism constantly fed me false thoughts, which caused me to shop, and it served up a sense of embarrassment when I wanted to wear clothes from my chock-full walk-in closet. My newfound awareness has made me realize that all this was a manifestation of my insecurity-fuelled perfectionism. Now I'm going to do something about it!"

The rules for this epic year-long battle were:

Only underwear, bras, and socks could be purchased.

No second-hand clothing shopping.

No shopping if travelling out of the country.

I could borrow clothing. My co-workers, family members, and friends could lend or gift me clothes.

If I thought I absolutely needed a new piece of clothing, I could appeal to the clothing council — my husband. (None of my appeals were granted!)

I put in the hard work, hustled, and stayed diligent. My hardcore training regime included the following strategies and tactics:

Stay out of the boutiques. That way, I wasn't tempted to try anything on, and so I wasn't tempted to purchase.

When browsing online, I kept my credit card a safe distance away.

I developed a relationship with a tailor. Adjusting some of my clothes made me feel as if I had something new. Clothes were repaired to ensure that they lasted all year.

I trained myself to change my attitude and to be more cautious and gentler with my clothes instead of treating them as disposable items. Before, if I got bored with outfits, I discarded them and bought something new.

The stakes of this fight were high, and I knew my training would pay off short and long term. My four-year long-term goal was to set foot on all seven continents before I turned forty. Two continents were still on my list, South America and Antarctica, and I was determined to make this dream a reality. But I needed to save, not spend. Perfectionism wasn't going to hold me back!

The words of American professional heavyweight boxer and social justice activist Mohammad Ali strengthened me. "He who is not courageous enough to take risks will accomplish nothing in life".

I had a game plan and with twelve rounds of action, I wanted a win!

## ROUND 1

I came out swinging during January and February and showed effective aggressiveness by window shopping and swooning over pieces . . . from a distance. I imagined how an outfit would look on me and pair with something in my closet. This curbed the endorphins surging through my veins. It was an electric feeling!

## ROUND 2

Perfection came back hard and almost KO'd me. I wanted to sucker punch and play dirty when I was travelling in Italy with my brother. So many unique boutiques and leather shoe shops were calling my name! My limits were being tested each day in this fashionable country, but I stayed above board and true to the rules. Instead of giving in, I became my brother's fashion advisor, guiding and coaching him on his purchases of shoes, jackets, and shirts.

## ROUND 3

Coming into the summer months saw me on the ropes. Summer is my favourite fashion season and I adore nothing more than pretty dresses, cute flats, and flirty skirts! Perfectionism knew this and demonstrated Ring Generalship, winning points with the judges. It was a trying time.

## ROUND 4

I continued to roll with the punches and stay in the fight. I gave myself credit for how far I had come as I intimately know how tough and slimy this opponent really is.

## ROUND 5

With each uppercut punch and body blow to Perfectionism, I could see things clearer. I knew my determination to win, sheer grit, and focus were paying off. We were going toe-to-toe, and I felt I was winning. I couldn't get cocky though, so I stayed focused while throwing my biggest combination of punches.

### ROUND 6

The Flawless Wonder delivered perfectly placed left and right hooks in the Fall as I pined for boot season and comfy sweaters. I was feeling winded, but I was half-way through this fight, and I wasn't giving up!

### ROUND 7

I wore Perfectionism down by not getting worked up about finding the perfect outfit for that wedding, this going-away party, or that Christmas soirée. Beat it!

### ROUND 8

I was flexing a new muscle in this fight. My conditioning was paying off, as I didn't care if people saw me in the same outfit. This was an immense blow to Perfectionism. I was gaining momentum and wanted hard core revenge, as many times I was deflated and fell into an uncontrollable tailspin. But I was ready to fight to the final round.

### ROUND 9

I could almost see the end of the fight, but I needed inspiration and refuelling. I ate inspirational quotes for breakfast, lunch, and dinner. Fictional sports boxer Rocky Balboa motivated me — "Every champion was once a contender who refused to give up". That was me.

### ROUND 10

I realized how much energy I was saving by not putting the effort into finding that "perfect outfit". But understanding it didn't bring me joy. I channeled this new energy back into the fight!

## ROUND 11

As I entered the championship rounds, I felt I had learned my lesson in the ring but that I couldn't let my guard down. It takes twelve rounds to win, and I had to fight until the final bell. I channelled my energy by donning the shirt of eight-time hometown World Champion boxer Jelena Mrdjenovich. I instantly felt stronger. Jelena has been described as sure, sharp, potent and a true world class boxer and competitor. All things I wanted to be! I was energized.

## ROUND 12

I knew I had a good chance at winning. The momentum in the ring went back and forth, but in this last round I felt my opponent lose power, and I sensed I was the ringmaster. I couldn't be sure until I heard the results, but I had fought each round with true will and determination. No matter what the score card said and who won the title, I was happy with my performance.

I hand it back to the announcers and judges.

"As the final bell rings three times, we close the electrifying boxing ring down. What a riveting fight filled with style and substance! We have been thoroughly entertained by the performance of these two. Both fighters have shown that they deserve to be here. Perfectionism has met a worthy adversary. It is a thrill and exhilaration to watch any battle of human behaviour, and this one has not disappointed in any way!

"The fight is too close to call, and so we wait for the scorecards from the three judges.

"The first scores the bout at 116–112 in favour of The Rainbow Puncher.

"The second also favours The Rainbow Puncher by 115–113

"Aaaaaaaaaaaaand the last judge gives the fight to The Rainbow Puncher by an identical score, 115–113

"The winner by unanimous decision and our NEW World Champion, Jalene E. Murphy! She has finally earned her first title! Put your hands together and make some noise for The Rainbow Puncher!

"There is a reason boxing is described as the theatre of the unexpected! Tonight we have witnessed an upset, and fans around the world have not only been entertained but wowed! Jalene E. Murphy has finally beat perfectionism and put it in its place! The Flawless Wonder isn't perfect after all!

"Good night, and thank you all for tuning in!"

\*\*\*

How did my twelve-month freeze on buying clothes change my habits? Since I wasn't adding anything new to my closet, I became aware of the clothes I had and clothes I wasn't wearing. This allowed me to pair down and streamline my wardrobe. I also identified which staple pieces were missing. When I resumed regular shopping, I looked for classic and better-quality options and avoided fast fashion or trendy pieces. My priority was interchangeable items that could be paired with other pieces in my closet. I also tried to purchase season-less clothing. I gained more understanding of myself as to why I had an urge to shop and now was at peace to wear what is in my closet. Shopping doesn't bring me happiness as I once thought, and I no longer rely on comments from others on the outfits I wear to fuel my esteem. The odd time when I am drawn to a piece of clothing or pair of shoes, I simply pause and reflect before I spend. I've lost the anxious need to shop and feeling of instant gratification after a purchase. After twelve months, I am comfortable with myself and the clothes I'm in.

*Chapter 4*

# COMING HOME

**PART ONE
CONNECTIONS**

Mimikwas (mi-mi-kway-s) - Butterfly.

Butterflies represent a new beginning; open to change, patience, being light and free. A form breaking through one's boundaries to free their spirit.

Orange represents change, movement and transformation.

It is 1999, and I am nineteen years old.

Growing up in a Catholic home, I attended a Catholic Church and a Catholic school. I wasn't exposed to any positive or affirming messages concerning sex. Instead, the adults in my life instilled in me the certainty that if I had sex before marriage, I would go to hell. Sex before marriage was a sin — sin, sin, sin. Abstinence motivated by fear was the ticket. No conversation. It was that black and white.

When I met my first boyfriend and engaged in the intimacy of a relationship and getting to know my body, I wrote in my journal, "I don't want to lose my soul. I don't want to be soulless. I want to be with God and the angels. I don't want to lose my spot. I believe in God, and I want to go to heaven. I want to do what's right. I want to live the life that He wants. I love Him. I want to be a child of God".

It is 2001, and I am twenty-one years old.

I have fallen madly in love with Josh. I want to be with him sexually. Wanting to express myself sexually was coming from a place of love. I struggled with the idea that, according to the Church, this was wrong and damning. Would I really go to hell? Would I lose my soul? Perfectionism reminded me I wasn't being the perfect Catholic if I didn't follow the no-sex-before-marriage rule. I wrote in my journal,

> What if the rules were made up? What am I waiting for? I feel conflict in my head. Maybe God didn't create these rules. But what if he did? I'm starting to question what I believe, and I'm so confused. I'm questioning the Lord. I feel less attached to Him and more attached to Josh. I feel Josh and I can get through anything. And I'm doubting my relationship with God. Why am I? For twenty-one years I believed without questioning, and now this disbelief

> has set in. I don't know what to believe. I'm scared to ask God. I feel like a traitor. I feel lost and not sure where to turn. I told Josh we should just get married, but I don't think that is going to solve my problem. I always thought I would wait for marriage to be with Josh, but after tonight I'm not sure what to think. I feel out of sync with my life. I didn't even say grace before I had dinner, because I didn't know what to believe anymore.

I held onto a belief that had been ingrained in me and said no to sex before marriage so many times. Now, I was feeling like a hypocrite for even thinking of taking a different route.

I am thankful that I didn't wait to have sex for the first time until Josh and I were married. I didn't lose my soul. My entire identity had been wrapped up in beliefs about my virginity, but I learned they were not true. Josh was patient and supportive as I broke down those faith based beliefs and began questioning the reality of the unrelenting Catholic teaching I had been subjected to. I realized it had moulded my brain, and that I had grown up disconnected from my body. Because I was taught not to engage in sex before marriage, it never crossed my mind to try out different ways of being sexual. I wasn't given an option.

It is 2004, and I am twenty-four years old.

I married Josh in the Catholic Church. It was one of the happiest days of my life.

The Catholic Church preached several messages. Some made complete sense to me, such as the power of unconditional love and forgiveness. However, the Church also preached that being gay was wrong and a sin. This made little sense to me, and internally I pushed back — if God created men and women in his likeness, then he obviously created gay people as well. Years after I left the Catholic Church, I still felt brainwashed. I was slowly unthawing from decades of messaging based on fear, guilt, and shame.

It is 2010, and I am thirty years old.

I am happily married to Josh, my loving, supportive, and patient husband. I feel positive about my body and using it in a sexual way — the guilt and shame of past years has finally dissipated. However, over the course of our marriage, I was becoming curious about being with a woman sexually, and now I was ready to have this experience without Catholic guilt, remorse, or judgement.

For my thirtieth birthday, I planned to celebrate with a two-and-a-half-month trip through Turkey, Syria, Jordan, Egypt, and Greece. I had worked hard and saved, and now I was about to leave and meet a friend in Istanbul, where my adventure would start. Because of my growing curiosity about having sex with a woman, Josh and I agreed that if an opportunity presented itself, I could take advantage of it. We had shaped our marriage the way we wanted it to be, and within it I had a lot of support.

I did meet a woman, Eve. It was springtime, and my travelling companion and I were staying at a hostel in the Turkish coastal town of Olympos. Eve was drinking Efes beer, and so I ordered the same, and we sat by the outdoor campfire and talked for hours about what we did for a living and what had brought us here. Then we went to a local nightclub where we danced closely. I felt the energy between us. As we walked back to the hostel, I extended my hand to see if Eve would take it. . . . She did.

Eve asked me if I wanted to kiss her. A pound of butterflies wrestled in my stomach as I was super nervous and shy, and very unsure of myself in relation to women. But I mustered up the courage and said yes. We drew into each other, and I touched her jet-black hair and caressed her curvy hips. Eve's soft, sensual touch electrified me under the star-lit night sky. It was a kiss that rocked my world. Neither of us had our own room and so, in total darkness, I ended up loving her in a change room at the hostel.

Being with Eve was easy to understand and hard to comprehend. Connecting to her feminine ways and energy was sublime and mysterious, and I felt a whole new world opening up to me.

Even though I had just met Eve, I experienced a feeling of wholeness and a sense of familiarity — a rebirth of something lost. My time with her unleashed something that couldn't be taken back. I was in a different country on a different continent, and yet being with her felt like I was coming home.

However, the experience also threw me into disarray. I was married and in love with my husband, and this encounter thousands of miles from home was challenging my identity as a heterosexual, married woman and ushering in a whole range of feelings. I wrote in my journal, "I don't think I'm gay. It just doesn't add up — I don't think I'm bisexual either". The Catholic teachings of my youth resurfaced, and

I became confused about "right" and "wrong". I tried to categorize my time with Eve as either "gay" or "not gay", as I thought it had to be one or the other. I wrote again, "I am sure I am not gay. I would just like to see her again".

I am back in Canada, married and still loving our life together, but I was yearning to be with Eve. Loving her had truly changed and challenged my long-held perspective of self, and I was at a loss as to what to do. Josh was uncertain how to comfort me.

I had questions.

Can I love two people at a time? Can I love each one differently?

Can I have two romantic connections at one time?

Can I enjoy the pleasures of touch without having to define it as straight or gay?

My encounter with Eve made me more sensitive to women and their beauty, and I began to tune into my sensual nature. It was all about softness and a lingering, feminine touch and expressive fingertips. Gradually I concluded that sex with a woman was a more inclusive experience.

All this rocked me to the core, and I drifted in uncharted waters — alone in my sexual ocean trying to sort it all out. I felt my sexual and sensual side tied so closely to my identity and image of myself. How do I navigate it all?

It is 2012, and I am thirty-two years old.

For the past two years, I have done my best to push the feelings of yearning for Eve under the rug — to forget about her. One evening I watched a movie, *The Best Exotic Marigold Hotel*, and I was stirred by the theme of lost love. Even though I had no contact details for Eve — just her first name and the industry she worked in, I became determined to reconnect with her. After many, many, internet searches, I landed on her blog.

Still unsure, I emailed her asking if she was Eve whom I had met on the Turkish Coast a few years earlier. She replied she was. My heart was pounding! I just couldn't comprehend how someone halfway around the world could have such an effect on me. I had to figure out why. Josh was extremely supportive and encouraged me to see her again so I could gain more understanding of myself. Six months after reconnecting with Eve by email Josh dropped me off at Edmonton International Airport for the first of several flights that would take me to Istanbul. I could tell he was nervous, and so I reassured him — and myself — that it was only this one woman, and I just had to see it through. There was no question that I would come back because I was completely in love with him.

Being with Eve again felt exactly as it had two and a half years earlier.

I turned thirty-three in Istanbul.

It is 2015, and I am thirty-five years old.

I changed my name from my married name back to my maiden name to help me feel more settled within myself. As I talked to my psychologist — I had been seeing her every six months for the past several years — I struggled with the words "connection" and "restlessness". I didn't think it had anything to do with our marriage. I just had to find the problem so I could fix it.

It is 2018, and I am thirty-eight years old.

In late May I was at a crossroads. I was living for two weeks at the home of my boss who was on holiday. I needed space from Josh to think about my marriage — should I stay or leave. I told Josh that I thought we should get a divorce as I was no longer fulfilled by our marriage. It was not clear to me that this was because I liked women — I just knew that I was not happy and thought that the only way to happiness was by getting a divorce. In the end we tried to kick-start our relationship by reworking a few areas.

In July I was in Kelowna, British Columbia, for a week's vacation with my brother. It was delightful — hot summer weather, side-of-the road fresh fruit and vegetables stands, sun-kissed orchards and wineries, long lakes filled with all kinds of boats, beach volleyball courts, and promenades to stroll down while licking ice cream cones. One chill beach day I was soaking up the summer vibe when things aligned for me. Afterwards it reminded me of a vision test at an optometrist's office. The doctor clicks the machine, different lens appear in front of my eyes, and the letters on the wall chart go from blurry to crystal clear and back to blurry. My job is to tell the optometrist when the letters come into sharp focus.

For years my vision — my understanding of my sexuality — had been blurry, but things changed for me that day, and my vision became crystal clear. As I looked at the women and men on the beach, everything came into focus. Both were easy on the eyes, but it was the women who held my interest, my gaze, and my intrigue. I bashfully began to study women, and I found their movements, gestures, and frames fascinating and nothing short of beautiful. That was the day I realized it wasn't just one woman in Turkey — I liked women, and they held my interest 100 percent.

This revelation was devastating as I was married to Josh, and we both loved each other. When I got home, I sobbed, "I think I like women". Josh reassuringly chuckled, saying, "Of course you do". But neither of us really understood the ramifications of my discovery.

At this time, I was deep into reading books on marriage, affairs, and sexuality. Two of them, *Living Two Lives: Married to a Man & In Love with a Woman*, by Joanne Fleisher; and *Married Women Who Love Women*, by Carren Strock, became lifelines for me. I felt as if I was reading about my thoughts and feelings and what I had already experienced.

Fleisher identified two concerns that resonated with me. "How will this attraction affect my marriage and family," she asked, "and how will it affect me as a person and my sexual identity? These two issues become intertwined, each affecting the other. At this stage, the challenge is to tolerate the ambiguity of not having the answers, perhaps the most difficult aspect of the process" (3).

The last few months had already been stressful, with my mom losing weight and finally being diagnosed with colitis. Dad, who was continuously fainting because of his heart condition, had a pacemaker put in, and my mother-in-law was diagnosed with cancer and was undergoing radiation treatment followed by surgery. I was unsettled in my marriage, and I was also beginning to understand that I had to deal with some childhood trauma. And finally, I was trying to figure out who I was — my sexual identity. It was all overwhelming, and I wasn't sure that my marriage would survive. My right thumb froze from the stress.

Fleisher identified the role that fear was playing in my life. "Fear is a huge barrier," she wrote. "Without a question, it takes enormous courage to confront your sexuality as an adult when so much is at stake; your marriage, your children, your entire way of life" (XV). I was full of fear, but I knew I also couldn't live a lie. Was I truly and completely gay? If so, I would be the first gay person in my immediate and extended family.

Both Fleisher and Strock affirmed I had to take brave steps to find out. "You are starting a journey of self-examination, a reconstruction of your core identity," Fleisher stated. "The journey is frightening because of how much you might have to give up" (2, x). Strock observed, "It takes a tremendous amount of strength for a married woman who discovers she loves women to explore what is happening to her. And even more courage to acknowledge that she does have options and begin her search for them" (37).

This all made complete sense to me. I was desperately trying to figure out how gay I was — 50 percent? 60 percent? Was I so gay that I had to leave my marriage? If I chose to leave, I would be giving up not only the life I had known, but the security and love of my husband. Was it worth the risk?

# PART TWO
# MENTAL HEALTH AND HEALING

Muskwa (musk-wa) - Bear

Bear represents courage. Bears remind us that we have mental and moral strength stored within ourselves.

Purple represents self-knowledge, deepening the understanding of our inner self.

*"I hate you. I want to leave you for dead. Leave you slaughtered on the playground. To never return and humiliate me again. I want to cut you down to pieces and let you rot in your wrongness and in your inconsideration".*

I wrote these words in an exercise as an adult to help me understand the depth of hurt I was experiencing and to acknowledge the anger I was holding towards those who hurt me over two decades ago.

During 2018, at about the same time as I realized that I truly liked women, I began to deal with the psychological wounds I had received when I was a thin and tiny young girl — all of forty-five pounds — in grades 5 and 6. I was aggressively bullied, as my psychologist called it, for something I couldn't change and had no control over — I was flat-chested. As a result, I felt that something was wrong with me, and that I wasn't good enough.

As an adult, it took me some time to make these connections. I started to notice that my shoulders were up around my neck and had to remind myself to lower them. I found myself always tense. It felt like I was on constant guard; I was extremely short-tempered and defensive, and I shook and became hot when Josh asked me questions I didn't have the answers to. When I finally connected the dots, it brought me back to that time and place. Hurtful words flung at me by boys on the playground. Insults that cut deep, stinging my entire body and humiliating me to my very core. I choked back anger, I fought back tears, and I did everything I could to keep from turning bright red. I wasn't going to give my tormentors the satisfaction of seeing how hurt I was, and so I confronted them and told them to shut up. At the time, bullying was not seen as a problem, and children weren't encouraged to ask adults for help and support. Instead, the message to girls my age was, "Boys tease you because they like you". And so, I never told anyone about the bullying and toughed it out alone.

In the summer and fall of 2018, I was seeing my psychologist monthly, trying to deal with the bullying as well as the unravelling of my sexuality and identity as a straight woman and my heterosexual marriage. When I asked her about the time frame for getting myself "back on track", she smiled supportively and said, "Sorry J, there isn't a time frame". The needed healing of a mental health challenge cannot be assigned a definite recovery time. It's not like a broken bone or a visible wound. During this time, Peter Levine's *Waking the Tiger: Healing Trauma* was a saving grace. Levine taught me that "traumatic effects are not always apparent immediately following the incidents that caused them. Symptoms can remain dormant, accumulating over years or even decades. Then, during a stressful period, they can show up without warning"(45). This was true for me.

In late August I started sleeping in a tank top and underwear — until then I had slept naked. I also stopped having a sexual relationship with Josh. Something didn't feel right within, and I told him, "I just don't feel safe". However, we showered and bathed together, and I still loved his hugs. He was only ever a supportive and loving husband. Nothing was clear during this time — did my problems stem from the sexual unravelling or the bullying? I didn't know.

Josh wanted to know what was happening with us and our marriage, and I didn't have a clear answer. Sometimes, when he pressed me for answers, my responses made no sense. Hot and shaking, I reverted to the survival techniques I had developed when I was in elementary school — "You're disgusting!" and, "Why can't you get it through your thick skull. . . ?" I didn't recognize that it was Josh I was saying these deeply hurtful things to.

I have always been an extrovert and involved in different activities, but during this time I curbed my social schedule. My energy was low, and I slept a lot. I spent plenty of my time in nature and a lot of time by myself. I still worked full time, which helped maintain some normalcy in my life and provided a welcome distraction from the processing.

Everyone at work was supportive. My boss, to whom I had confided "I'm not 100 percent straight", encouraged me to keep my appointments with my therapist, and my co-workers gave me space on the days I needed to be left alone and unconditional love on the days I needed closeness.

Still, it was difficult. At times when I was on the phone, I had to put clients on hold while I gathered myself, and I often left the office for a short walk, taking in deep breaths of fresh air. Some days I felt raw and exposed from head to toe, and during other days I left meetings to cry privately and shake to release my anger. And then there were days when I got into my car after work and couldn't turn on the radio as I needed silence — to be wrapped in a cocoon of silence.

The all-encompassing anger I was processing was fierce — anger bottled up from what had happened all those years ago. It swirled inside of me, raging, and then seeped out of my pores. The toxic energy was so powerful that at times I felt I could light up San Francisco. In order to keep it circulating and not bubbling over, I swam or walked fast on a treadmill.

One morning, as I was completing my get-ready-for-work routine, I looked at the padded bra on the bed. "NO! I will not put you on!" Every day for years I had worn padded bras, push-up bras, water bras, or air bras. I had started each and every day by reinforcing that I wasn't good enough. Well . . . no more! That was the day I became aware of what I was doing and stopped pretending to be who I wasn't and started loving who I was. That was the day I stopped wearing padded bras.

## MODERN DAY COURAGE

During the autumn, I read several books on trauma, abuse, and healing to get a better understanding of what I was going through and develop a vocabulary that could describe what I was experiencing. One book asked the reader to complete a sentence as a way of exploring denial. "I'm afraid to admit that I was traumatized in this way because _____." I wrote, "it's trivial". But the bullying I had experienced wasn't — it was affecting my whole life, and I couldn't downplay it any further. There was no way around it. I had to face this deep wound, and I had to be vulnerable. I didn't want to admit they had hurt me because I thought it showed weakness, and the last thing I wanted was to feel weak. Weakness meant those boys had won. I wanted to be seen as invincible and strong and to shield and protect my heart from being hurt any further. But admitting I was hurt was a critical step in my healing journey.

I struggled to find a word to describe my past experiences and what I was experiencing in the present. I came to understand that word was trauma.

In *Waking the Tiger; Healing Trauma*, Levine identifies the four components that are present to some degree in any traumatized person. I experienced them all and can explain them. Hyperarousal manifests itself in times of stress as a racing heart, quick and shallow breathing, muscular twitchiness, difficulty sleeping, agitation, and anxiety. Constriction creates a tensing and tightening of our system, including our visual field, as we get ready to protect ourselves. Freezing is the immobility that comes from overwhelming helplessness and fear. And finally, dissociation occurs in many ways but always involves a split in connection, for example, between the past and the present. It refers to a disconnection in the continuity of a person's embodied sense of self.

Of these four, my experience with dissociation scared me the most. It was something I never knew could even happen — a few moments where normal time and space didn't exist. Josh and I were in the kitchen one evening in late October, and he was asking me questions I couldn't answer — where was our relationship going, and what was going to happen to us as a couple. I didn't know what to say because I had no idea what was happening to me.

I was feeling pressured to answer these challenging questions, and when that happens, I want to escape. But Josh blocked me, as he wanted to continue the conversation. I kicked and hit him — I wanted him to let me leave. Then I started throwing things at him from the kitchen counter and holding out my arm, telling him to stay away and that I didn't feel safe. My body stayed in the present, but my mind was transported back to grades 5 and 6 and the playground at Sacred Heart School in Wetaskiwin, back to a time when I didn't feel safe. I was detached from my immediate surroundings, from the condo I knew so well, and from my current 2018 reality.

I then ran into the bathroom and locked the door and told Josh to call his mom for support. I was not thinking rationally as my system was on high alert and ready to protect myself at all costs. My emotions were in a state of upheaval and because I didn't feel safe, I had to get out of the condo as fast as possible. Meanwhile, dear Josh was trying to calm me down and pleading with me to stay, but I couldn't. I unlocked the bathroom door and made a beeline for the front door, leaving Josh crying, upset, and at a complete loss as to what had just happened. I went straight back to the place where I was staying and put a hot water pack on my kidneys. This calmed my body — I felt as if I had weathered a storm and found a safe harbour. The next day, I was physically exhausted and completely spent.

When I read *Waking the Tiger; Healing Trauma* and realized that other people had experienced the same thing, I felt better. I was not alone, and I experienced a sense of belonging.

In early November, about two weeks after I experienced dissociation, I moved out of our condo. My therapist had suggested I do this so that I could have more space to work through the effects of my childhood trauma. As well, I was dealing with my sexuality and whether I should end my marriage. A few weeks earlier I had written in my journal for the first time, "I'm gay". For the next several months I bounced around different apartments and houses that my boss helped me find, sometimes paying rent and other times house sitting. My boss was incredibly supportive, even contributing financially to the cost of my therapy. I was still attracted to women, and I allowed myself to look at them without berating my inner being. Women were who I was most attracted to, and I gradually realized that I was not in love with Josh as a husband.

During that time, I worked with my therapist and tried various techniques to heal my trauma. Through Somatic Experiencing, a body-oriented approach that helps the nervous system release bound trauma and stress energy, I was able to initiate healing and re-integrate lost and fragmented portions of my essential self. When my thumb froze, I found a rolfer to help me regain feeling. As he worked on my body, I asked him to avoid working anywhere near my breast area — it was 100 percent off limits.

I tracked my healing and broke it up into three-month blocks. Every day I journaled in order to follow the small improvements in my thoughts and feelings. It was a way to feel better about myself. I also found strength in the Alex Janvier painting "One Day at a Time" and reminded myself to do only that. Looking too far into the future was overwhelming.

Since I wanted complete freedom from trauma in relation to my mind-body connection, I sought different ways to heal and decided to work with a somatic sex educator who works with the body to nurture and heal sensual self. We connected the breast area through touch, safe boundaries, and clear communication back to my mind. It was a way to liberate my mind and body completely. It was a practice of leaving shame behind and truly owning my sexuality and feelings of deservability. I also started talking and sharing with others about being bullied as a young girl. This included giving a speech on my experiences at a Toastmaster gathering. Being able to talk and share with others has been a form of healing.

# PART THREE
# ALWAYS AND FOREVER

Mooswa (moos-wa) - Moose

Moose represents inner beauty. Moose reminds us to take pride in ourselves; do not need to feel ashamed or pressured to be anything but your true self.

Pride colours are displayed on the Moose while on a "gender" role coloured backdrop.

By early March 2019, I had to make a heartbreaking decision.

Months of therapy had helped me understand I was at a fork in the road that represented my life. Choosing the right meant staying in my marriage while turning left started with a divorce before journeying on. For months there wasn't a clear indicator in my mind on what to do. Later I realized that my heart had already figured it out, but I wasn't paying attention — I didn't value my heart's input.

Our fifteen-year wedding anniversary was just over a month away. We had grown up together, walked beside each other for eighteen years, and forged a loving marriage. We were each other's biggest supporters, and we encouraged each other to grow and learn. We believed we could create and shape our marriage the way we wanted it to be.

During the last eight years, Josh had been extremely supportive and stood by my side as I was unravelling and coming to understand the complexity of my sexuality. He had showed me love and compassion when I couldn't give those things to myself, and he was patient and gracious when my actions and words were skewed and tainted from hurt and pain caused by the bullying I endured as a young girl. Josh never left my side, even in the face of huge unknowns. This is the measure of a man among men. It was Josh's unwavering love and support that made it so difficult and heartbreaking to arrive at the distressing decision to leave our marriage. Why would I throw away true love?

Deep feelings of selfishness, sadness, shame, and guilt overwhelmed me when I thought about the wedding vows I had made all those years ago — vows I was now contemplating breaking. I am fiercely loyal, and reneging on my promise to be married till death do us part was difficult to come to terms with. I felt like a hypocrite. When I looked at photos of my Ukrainian grandparents up on my fridge, affectionately known as Baba and Gido, and specifically their wedding picture, I felt ashamed for not being able to "go the distance". Our family places a strong value on long-lasting marriages, and I wanted to be part of that legacy. The thought that I couldn't made me sad. At one point I wrote in my journal, "Wishing I could go back to how things were".

For the longest time, I was looking for the precise problem so I could come up with the solution to fix it. However, the longer I struggled, the more I realized that there wasn't anything that needed fixing. I was simply in the wrong relationship, and if I was going to be honest and trust myself, I had to make the tough decision to end my marriage. The arrangement of having a husband and a girlfriend suited some couples, but I knew it wouldn't work for me. I also knew that a divorce would devastate Josh, but I couldn't continue as I knew I would become resentful.

I didn't know where I would end up, but I did know that in order to be my fully complete known and sexual self, I had to go beyond my marriage and start living as a woman who wants, needs, and belongs with women. I had to shed the layers of Catholic Church guilt and shame for "not making my marriage work". And I had to forgive myself for not keeping the promise of "always and forever" and start learning to love and accept myself for wanting a girlfriend. I could no longer deny or punish myself for wanting something that so strongly aligned with my inner being.

Once I accepted this, my understanding of our marriage started to change — it had been successful, even though it did not possess longevity. I have since come to gauge the success of a relationship by how much one grows and blossoms as an individual and a couple and by how much love, care, support, and respect is present. Loving someone — in my case Josh — didn't mean I needed to stay married to him, and ending the marriage didn't discount the profound and positive impact we had on one another.

However, the months leading up to my asking Josh for a divorce in March were a time of mourning of what once was — the marriage I had once loved, cherished, and grown comfortable with. The quirky rituals, the inside jokes, and the ways we looked at each and knew the answer to a question without speaking. The way I knew how Josh's day had gone by the way he opened the door and dropped his keys on the table. I had fallen in love with Josh by the end of our first date, and since then we had had each other's back. Ending our marriage would break both our hearts and change our lives forever. This mourning continued well past July 2020, when the divorce became final.

One of the saddest, most heart wrenching days of my life was when I opened the door of the home I once cherished to ask the person I once loved so deeply for a divorce. It was a cool morning in March 2019, and as I had climbed each flight of stairs to the condo moments before, I had struggled with the heaviness in my heart. We talked for hours, and when I asked Josh to start thinking about his own plans and decisions, he replied he hadn't made a decision in eighteen years without me in mind. Every sentence between us carried weight. He eventually agreed to a divorce, even though he thought it was the wrong decision.

As I left the condo that afternoon, I wasn't sure where I was going to land. Among the many thoughts and emotions that overwhelmed me was the realization that I had lost my best friend — the person who had loved me at my worst and my best. However, somewhere deep inside I felt relieved to have taken the courageous and difficult first step. I had always felt strong, safe, and secure in my marriage, but now I realized I needed to find those things within myself. I had to stay strong, to believe, and to start living my new, true life. I didn't fully understand what that life would look like, but I knew I had taken the first step to finding out. That evening, I bought the smallest pair of leaf earrings. As I put them on, I sensed they represented inevitable change. Every autumn, leaves fall signalling a change of season. My new season was about to begin, and I was finally ready.

As my marriage drew to an end, I prepared to "come out" to my family and friends and let them know I was going to get a girlfriend. However, the prospect of deliberately dismantling the standard of perfection that I had held myself to and breaking the mould of how people viewed me — a heterosexual married woman — terrified me. The process has involved an unravelling of and sifting through of almost all my opinions and beliefs, trying to decide which were true for me — not the Catholic Church, not my parents, not society, but for me. It was difficult. I had always seen myself as a good girl, the "perfect" wife who kept her marriage vows, and now I would be a "divorcee".

How would my family members or any of my friends understand? No one in my family had strayed to from faith, and certainly none of them were gay. I had no gay friends, and there was no one close to talk to about what I was going through. I was still living a very straight life. To deliberately break this wide open, and for people to view me differently was hard to imagine and filled me with fear and anxiety — fear of rejection, fear of not being loved for who I was, and fear of losing connection with my family. In my head I painted the worst scenarios possible, and the resulting fear paralyzed me. As I struggled, I realized that the only one with the key to unlock that prison of fear I lived in was me.

Some months earlier I had confided in a trusted few, sharing my beliefs and feelings, and since then I slowly took action — baby steps worked best — that aligned with my true values. I devoured quotes by Rumi, Helen Keller, and Winston Churchill for weeks leading up to telling my parents that I was going to get a girlfriend. I hoped these strengthening insights would build up my courage and confidence and help me face this huge fear. When I finally broke the news, everyone reacted differently. Some were initially shocked but then became supportive. Others said they didn't have any problems with it because it was 2019. (Had it been ten years earlier, they would have reacted differently). And still others said they didn't completely understand but wanted to see me happy and so they supported my decision.

Such a fundamental transformation doesn't work like a band-aid that I could just pull off and *voilà* — I was now a woman leading a gay life. The initial recognition that I was not 100 percent straight was sometimes too much for my brain to comprehend, and my new identity was difficult to move into. At times I found the reshaping process to be immobilizing and suffocating. In the end, the change was a multitude of baby steps — a continual process of saying to myself that it was okay to look at pretty girls, and it was just as okay to say that I could still find men attractive.

With help from friends and family, I made both small and big steps. Later that spring, I attended my first queer film festival and visited my first gay bar. I felt so empowered when I had the courage to say to the coffee barista, "I like it here, and I want to bring a girlfriend for an espresso". In the months that followed, my confidence grew, and I enjoyed my first Pride picnic, bought my first Pride-forward rainbow sneakers, and proudly took part in the annual Pink

Shirt Day. In June 2020, a month after my divorce papers were signed, I spent time with a woman — an experience that confirmed I am where I belong.

# A HEARTFELT THANK YOU

To all those who helped me on my journey and helped me prepare this book, I am eternally grateful. I truly count my blessings.

My former husband Josh. For your love, support, and endless patience.

My boss Lesley Paull. For your guidance, love, and kindness.

My friends, especially Jess, Kayla, and E. You are my special earth angels.

My family and my Paull Travel work family. For accepting and loving me as I am.

DHB — my psychologist. For helping me get back on track!

Graem Monilaws — my rolfer. For your healing hands and bringing awareness to how strong the mind-body connection is.

Penelope Hagan — my somatic sex educator. For your nurturing help. www.soultouch.ca

Chris Chipak/Wapikihew @inchipakwetrust for the beautiful nature infused artwork that graces each chapter. Thank you for the education and collaboration!

Toastmaster International, Edmonton chapter, where I learned how to write the speeches that were the foundation for this book.

For editor Philip Sherwood of *lifewriters.ca* who was integral in shaping *Modern Day Courage* into a viable manuscript.

Everyone who encouraged me to write my story and who offered feedback. Your support made this book happen.

## THESE BOOKS HELPED LIGHT MY PATH.

Peter Levine, *Waking the Tiger: Healing Trauma*, North Atlantic Books, 1997

Joanne Fleisher, *Living Two Lives. Married to a Man and in Love with a Woman*, Lavender Visions Books: Philadelphia, 2011

Carren Strock, *Married Woman Who Love Woman*, Routledge, 2008

Caffyn Jesse's four books:

*Healers on the Edge*, erospirit, 2017

*Orientation: Mapping Queer Meanings*, erospirit, 2004 and 2015

*Science for Sexual Happiness*, erospirit, 2016

*Erotic Massage for Healing and Pleasure*, erospirit, 2015

Tim Bradshaw, *Healing the Shame That Binds You*, Health Communications, 1988

Beverly Engel, *It Wasn't Your Fault*, New Harbinger Publications, 2015

Ellen Bass and Laura Davis, *The Courage to Heal*, HarperCollins Publishers, 2008

Sara Ahmed, *Living a Feminist Life*, Duke University Press, 2017 belle hooks, *all about love*, HarperCollins Publishers, 2001

Brené Brown, *Daring Greatly,* Penguin Random House, 2012

Doc Childre and Deborah Rozman, *Transforming Anger*, New Harbinger Publications,

Jaclyn Friedman, *What You Really Really Want*, Seal Press, 2011

Emily Nagoski, *Come As You Are*, Simon & Schuster Paperbacks, 2015

The Lazaris Material, www.lazaris.com

Printed in the USA
CPSIA information can be obtained
at www.ICGtesting.com
LVHW072102250924
792135LV00040B/215

9 781039 161337